BE BRAVE.

Second Edition

BIG POWERFUL MOVE INSIDE

Handle WITH COURAGE

Karen Rochester

Illustrated by **Kat Chadwick**

Be Brave
Second Edition

Written by Karen Rochester
Illustrated by Kat Chadwick

First published 2011
Second edition published January 2020

ISBN: 978-0-6487493-0-1 (sbk.)

© 2020 Karen Rochester
www.bebravebook.com

A catalogue record for this book is available from the National Library of Australia

Editor, Riima Daher (first edition)
Book design by Adam Laszczuk (first edition)
Additional design by Steve Horton at scoutcreative.com.au (second edition)

ACKNOWLEDGEMENTS

Without the love, support, guidance, assistance and positive feedback, especially from my husband, my family, friends, therapists and specialist doctors, *Be Brave* may never have become a reality.

I am very fortunate and truly grateful to everyone who has supported me and helped me come to terms with the traumas I have experienced. My hope is that *Be Brave* will provide enough encouragement for the reader to seek and find the help they need to manage the difficult times in their life.

Karen

Life is best when it's enjoyable and fun,
but it isn't always like that and some things that happen
don't make sense.

Sometimes bad things happen to people.

There may come a time when something bad comes into your life
and you won't know what to do about it ...

You might try all of your usual tricks to make it disappear and all of your clever fighting moves to make it go away.

But if none of them work, you might start to feel helpless; like there is nothing you can do to make things better, like there's no way out.

You might feel the worst you've ever felt.

But there IS something you can do.

Even when you're sure you've tried everything.

Especially when you are sure that there isn't anything else
that can work.

There is ALWAYS one more thing you CAN do.

If you're brave enough ...

There are many different ways to be brave.

You can be brave by SHOWING something that you have made,
or learned how to do, even though you might be shy,
or worried that someone might laugh.

Sometimes it means TRYING something new, or different,
or slightly unusual, even though it makes you feel nervous.

Or DEFENDING someone, or something you care about.

You can be brave by SAYING something to a person about their behaviour when they are doing something wrong.

Or OWNING UP to something you did, even though you know you might be punished.

You may be able to remember a time when you have been brave already.

Every single person on the planet has to be brave at least once in their life, no matter who they are, how old they are, or how strong they are.

Being brave is about having the courage to do the best thing, even when it's hard and especially when you're scared to do it.

One of the hardest times to be brave is when someone has hurt you.

It's especially hard to be brave if a person has hurt you and you don't know what to do about it.

If someone has harmed you, they may have made you feel pain by hurting your body.

They might have said cruel things, or threatening things, or frightening things.

They might have forced you to do something you didn't want to.

They might have told lies about you that really hurt, or taken something that was yours without asking.

The person who harmed you may have hurt you once,
or more than once, in one way, or many ways.

This person might still be hurting you.

No one has the right to hurt your body, or your feelings.

No one has the right to hurt your family, or your friends, or your pets, or your things.

No one is allowed to hurt another person, no matter who they are, or how old they are, or how important they are.

The person who has hurt you has done something very wrong.

It feels awful to be hurt by someone.

After a person has hurt you,
you might start to notice some changes in yourself.

You might FEEL all kinds of different feelings.

You might feel very angry.

You might be sad, or scared.

Some people feel sick, or have the feeling of 'butterflies' in their stomach.

You may not feel like eating, or you might eat more than usual.

You might have bad dreams.

Pictures of what happened might suddenly pop up in your head while you're awake and they might have strange feelings attached to them.

You might feel like you're alone, like no one could possibly understand how you're feeling, or what you're going through.

You might feel like no one could do anything to help you even if they wanted to.

But try not to worry.

It's normal to have these sorts of feelings if someone has hurt you.

Being hurt might cause you to ACT differently.

You might cry a lot.

You might say, or do things that you wouldn't normally say, or do.

You might become quieter than usual, or louder than usual.

You may be afraid to go to certain places.

You might find it hard to concentrate, or get any work done.

You may not feel like doing some of your usual activities anymore and it might get harder to get along with your friends as well as you used to.

You might find yourself doing some things without thinking and not know why you did them.

You might even find yourself getting into trouble more often.

S ome people, especially those around you every day, might notice these changes in you and ask you what's wrong.

You might say something like, "nothing", or "I don't know", because you don't know what else to say.

Being hurt can make you act differently, even if you don't mean to.

It is natural and normal for your behaviour to change when someone has hurt you.

You might start to THINK differently too.

You might start to wonder if you are to blame for what happened to you.

You might think that there is something wrong with you.

You might even think that you are weak, or that you are being punished for something you did wrong.

NONE of these thoughts are right and NONE of them are true, but it's NORMAL to get your thoughts mixed up when you've been hurt.

It's natural to get confused about which thoughts are true and which ones are not when you are trying to work out;

'Why did this happen?'

It is hard to understand why a stranger,
or someone you don't know very well would hurt you.

It is especially hard to understand if the person who hurt you
is someone in your family, or a friend, or someone you spend
quite a lot of time with.

They could be a person who is trusted.

Someone you trusted.

No person is allowed to hurt another person for ANY reason, ever, so you are not to blame for what has happened to you, no matter what ANYONE tells you.

The person who hurt you knows they did something wrong, so they will do their best to make sure nobody finds out.

They may have warned you not to tell anyone about what they did.

They might even say that it's a secret between you and them.

They might say things to make you believe that something bad will happen if you ever tell anyone.

They want you to be scared so that you won't tell.

That's because they know that the only way they can get away with hurting you is if no one else ever finds out about it.

If someone has hurt you, there IS something you can do to help yourself.

There is one big, powerful move that just might work to make sure they don't hurt you, or anyone else again.

Only YOU can do it.

It is not easy to do, so you will need to be brave.

Would you like to know what it is?

You will need to TELL SOMEONE.

It takes a lot of COURAGE to tell someone that another person has hurt you, especially when you don't know the right words to use.

Maybe you feel uncomfortable, or too embarrassed to talk about it.

It's NORMAL and understandable to feel scared about telling someone what happened.

Feeling scared is always the first thing you feel when you have chosen to be brave.

So being scared is okay.

It means you're on your way ...

Even if you're scared, you can still find the courage within yourself to tell someone.

SAFE PERSON

The next thing you might feel when you choose to be brave is nervous.

That's because the second step towards being brave is taking a chance that what you do will work.

It feels much easier to take a chance when you know exactly what to do and exactly what will happen if you try.

Other times, like this, when you can't be absolutely sure
what will happen, it feels much harder to find the courage
to take such a chance.

You might worry that things could get worse if you tell,
or that the person who hurt you might get angry.

You might be scared that you could be hurt again,
or that someone else could get hurt.

SAFE PERSON

You might worry that people you care about might get upset.

You might be worried that you'll get in trouble.

You might even worry that no one will understand, or worse, that no one will believe you.

If you start worrying that these things could happen, you'll probably start to think that it would be better not to say anything at all.

At some stage, you might decide that it's just not worth taking the chance. That's to be expected and you're allowed to change your mind at any time.

It's possible that you might change your mind lots of times, back and forth, while you are deciding what to do.

That's what happens when people feel nervous about taking a big chance.

So even if you're feeling nervous, you can still be on your way to being brave.

You can still find the courage within yourself to tell someone.

There's just one important thing you should remember.

It's ALWAYS worth being brave and taking a chance when you are trying to make things BETTER!

Better

When you're ready to be brave and tell someone that you have been hurt, there are many people who can help you. You probably don't even realise how many people there are who can be there for you when you are scared and don't know what to do.

These people can find different ways to deal with problems, even when you feel absolutely sure they can't be fixed.

They can find ways to help you and keep you safe.

They can help you to feel better and think better.

They can help you to feel happy again.

When you are ready to be brave and talk about what happened to you, the person you pick to tell should be:

- An adult you believe you can trust.

- Someone who you can contact easily.

- Someone you believe will be able to support you.

- Someone who may be able to protect you from being hurt again.

This person is known as a "safe" person.

A safe person can be someone you know very well,
or a little,
or possibly someone you don't know at all.

Y ou will need to decide how you want to CONTACT the safe person you have chosen. You may like to talk to them alone, or you may like to have someone there with you for support.

You may choose to talk to them in person, but you can also choose to speak with them on the phone, or maybe even send them an email, a text or a message.

If you don't know how to begin, you could say something like: "Someone has hurt me. Can I please talk to you?"

How you decide to CONTACT and TELL a safe person what happened will depend on what works best for you.

TELL SOMEONE

DON'T tell Anyone

WRONG WAY, GO BACK

You might not be able to go through with telling a safe person everything the first time you try, or the second.

You might have to try a few times before you actually say what happened out loud, but keep trying.

No matter how many tries it takes, don't give up.

Tell a safe person that someone has hurt you.

The right person will listen.

They will believe you and they will help you.

Sometimes the first safe person you tell might ask you to
speak to another person they know.
Someone who can help you better than they can.

Try not to feel disappointed, or scared.

It's not because they don't want to help you;
it's quite the opposite.

It's because they believe this is the BEST way they can help you!

Sadly, there are a lot of other people who have been hurt like you.

That's why there are good, safe, strong adults whose role it is to help people like you who don't know what to do to stop the bad things that are happening to them.

They know how to keep people safe and they know how to help make bad feelings go away.

If your safe person suggests that you speak to one of these people, try not to worry, keep going and don't give up.

You may not know this other person very well, or maybe not at all, but if your safe person trusts them, then you can trust them too.

Telling this person might mean that you'll need to be brave all over again, but it also means that you will have ANOTHER person on your side and you'll be getting even MORE help!

The key to getting better starts with getting help.

And the key to getting help starts with BEING BRAVE!

So, if there does come a time in your life when something bad
happens that seems too big to beat on your own,
and you feel the worst you've ever felt and you're sure that there's
nothing you can do about it ... try to remember this:

There is ALWAYS one more thing you can do.

You will ALWAYS have that big, powerful move up your sleeve
and you will always have enough courage inside you to use it.

Can you remember what that is?

TELL SOMEONE.

BIG
POWERFUL
MOVE
INSIDE

Handle with courage

And let them help you make things BETTER.

Go on …

BE BRAVE.

Where to find a 'Safe person'

If you have been hurt, the 'safe person' you choose to tell may include: parents, teachers, friends, other relatives such as grandparents or aunties or uncles, parents of friends, a school counsellor, sports coach, activity leader, doctor, person of religion, or someone else you know and trust.

If you'd prefer to talk to someone else, you could contact any of the following:

Kids Help Line

Phone: **1800 55 1800**

www.kidshelp.com.au

Kids Helpline provides private and confidential, telephone and online (email) counselling services. It is a free service available 24 hours a day, 7 days a week specifically to young people aged between 5 and 25.

Lifeline

Phone: **13 11 14**

www.lifeline.org.au

Lifeline is a 24-hour telephone counselling service that is available to everyone. Staff are trained to provide help and support for many different emotional and social problems 24 hours a day, 7 days a week.

Beyond Blue

Phone: **1300 22 4636** (Information Line)

beyondblue.org.au

Beyond Blue provides information and support to help everyone in Australia achieve their best possible mental health, whatever their age and wherever they live. Their website provides extensive information on a wide range of mental health issues and available programs.

Reach Out!

au.reachout.com

Reach Out! is a web-based service that encourages young people to help themselves by providing information and fact sheets on a wide range of health and social issues. Reach Out! does not provide online, e-mail or telephone counselling services but has great information for all ages, especially young people aged between 14 and 25.

Bravehearts

Phone: **1800 272 831**

www.bravehearts.org.au

Bravehearts™ national Information and Support Line can be accessed by anyone wanting information or support relating to child sexual assault and exploitation. They are also active in advocacy, education, research and many community programs.

Child Abuse Prevention Service (CAPS)

Phone: **1800 688 009**

capsau.org

CAPS provide evidence-based educational programs, bespoke child safe organisation solutions and child rights consulting to build well-being, emotional resiliency with a goal to forever break the cycle of abuse.

Please visit www.bebravebook.com for more information.

www.ingramcontent.com/pod-product-compliance
Lightning Source LLC
LaVergne TN
LVHW072120070426
835511LV00002B/34